About the Author

Randi is an author and a poet who has written and published three books of poetry. She served in the USAF for five years, receiving an Honorable Discharge. Randi never lost interest in her desire to write and publish books. She lives in Alaska with her husband and four adult children and grandchildren. Having grown up in the foster care system with her siblings following the untimely deaths of their parents, Randi learned to use her interest in writing as a means of escape from her dysfunctional world of reality.

This... Is About Life... Lay Your Burdens Down

Randi Owens

This... Is About Life... Lay Your Burdens Down

Olympia Publishers
London

www.olympiapublishers.com
OLYMPIA PAPERBACK EDITION

Copyright © Randi Owens 2023

The right of Randi Owens to be identified as author of
this work has been asserted in accordance with sections 77 and 78 of
the Copyright, Designs and Patents Act 1988.

All Rights Reserved

No reproduction, copy or transmission of this publication
may be made without written permission.
No paragraph of this publication may be reproduced,
copied or transmitted save with the written permission of the publisher,
or in accordance with the provisions
of the Copyright Act 1956 (as amended).

Any person who commits any unauthorised act in relation to
this publication may be liable to criminal
prosecution and civil claims for damage.

A CIP catalogue record for this title is
available from the British Library.

ISBN: 978-1-80439-611-7

This is a work of fiction.
Names, characters, places and incidents originate from the writer's
imagination. Any resemblance to actual persons, living or dead, is
purely coincidental.

First Published in 2023

Olympia Publishers
Tallis House
2 Tallis Street
London
EC4Y 0AB

Printed in Great Britain

Dedication

I dedicate this book to my husband, Carlos. I am grateful to him for his willingness to support my dreams of writing. I feel blessed for the many years we've walked together as he's encouraged me to 'lay my burdens down'.

Acknowledgements

Thank you to my husband, Carlos, for his presence and support. Thank you to my children, Carlos Jr., Maria, Jose, and Xiomara, for always encouraging me when I want to give up and stop. And a special thank you to my best friend, Patti, for her encouragement, support, and willingness to help whenever I ask.

He Sat Beside Me

When I believed I could bear no more
He sat beside me on the cold and barren floor

Not a word was ever spoken
While in my head I heard, "Your spirit is unbroken"

There are times when my Faith waivers
But in that moment, I felt favored

We sat quietly as my tears flowed unchecked
He knew my heart and I knew I wasn't done yet

Together we looked out at the devastation that befell
I wanted to scream out… but my pain I withheld

When I believed I was all alone with no one to care
He sat beside me, and I knew that he was there

He was never far from me with an arm across my shoulder
I knew I could depend upon him as youth faded and I grew older

He sat beside me, with his presence forever calm
Not a word was spoken, with that I had no qualms

As we sat looking out at the world
I began to feel complete as my creativity unfurled

The peace I felt was all I had need of
He sat beside me, and I knew without words, that I was Loved

Smile for Me…

The voice was so clear
Smile for me my dear

I turned my head
As I lay in bed

With a smile on my face
There was calm without haste

My eyes were closed as I lay still
The smile came slowly, and I knew it was real

I wanted to open my eyes to see
Who had asked such a beautiful smile of me?

I opened my eyes, but no one was there
No one was in the bed, dark corner or sitting in the only chair

I continued to smile as I turned the lights on
The one that had been there was now long gone

There was no reason for me to continue that smile
But I held onto it for quite a long while

What a request, those three words
I'm glad it woke me, I'm happy I heard

Do I need a reason to smile when no one is there?
It simply felt good, and I didn't really care

The voice was so beautiful and clear
Open your eyes and 'smile for me my dear'

That Man Loves That Woman

He looks at her like she's all he needs
The love in his eyes is what she sees

Their partnership is forever strong
He'd never think to do her wrong

Her smile makes him feel like the man of her dreams
He looks forward to providing for her every means

Each day is fresh with few demands
He reaches for her as he lifts and kisses her hand

The laundry, meals and the dishes can wait
He'd much rather hold onto his beloved mate

He smiles to himself as he places his chin atop her head
Although they have much to do, he wants to just hold onto her instead

That man loves that woman as they walk hand-in-hand
He makes her breakfast and together they laugh as he kisses her again and again

He'd helped with the laundry and the housework was done
That man loves that woman as he plans events that are fun

She is his best friend, wife, and partner
He wants all to know just how much he truly loves her

As he opens the doors, pulls out her chairs and helps with her coat
He walks as if on air, feeling as if he could float

Smiling with pleasure throughout his deeds
Happy and content to provide for her needs.

That man loves that woman with all his heart…
He takes seriously his vow, until death do them part

Morning Delight

Standing straight in the morning light
With no relief for me in sight

Watching and waiting for her to move
Anxious to show I have something to prove

Reaching out to touch her hand
Knowing that she will understand

Aware that I have a short window of time
Gently reaching for what I believe to be mine

Grateful for the response and pleasant hold
Looking into beautiful eyes that make me bold

Filled with hope and genuine surprise
Anticipation and excitement I'm unable to disguise

My task complete, leaving joy in place
It was worth it to see the glow on her face

Feeling like I want to beat my chest
Instead, falling fast asleep after doing my best

The Good Father

Their mother is dead
Their welfare is on my head

Their precious lives are in my hands
They are mine to keep, love, cherish and understand

I will not fail these six babes of mine
I will honor their mother as our love still binds

A roof to secure them from the elements
Financial means to help pay the rent

Clothes on their backs to help keep them warm
Taking seriously my responsibility to keep them from harm

Food for their stomachs, making sure they're well fed
Kiss the cheeks of all six before putting them to bed

Feeling unprepared for the death that stole her away
Accepting of God's wisdom for allowing me to stay

Giving them away is not an option for me
Even the oldest one, not of my blood, is my child to keep

Working and spending time away is difficult for me to do
Because they are my babies and I trust few

Moving them from one home into another
Until realizing they are ill-treated or seen as too much trouble

Seeking someone else to provide for their care
Silently crying as I wish their mother was there

The good father worked hard, and he was unaware of the time
God called him home early and he had to leave his babies behind

Channeling Her Emotions

Channeling her emotions through a body that's fluid
Telling herself she knows she can do it

As you watch her perform such a beautiful art
You witness her voice through body and from heart

Small of stature and fragile to look upon
Strength displayed from the start until she's done

Moving like there's no one else there
Holding your attention as she dances with care

Channeling her emotions as she moves across the stage
Drawing out each challenge as if moving through a maze

Lifting a single leg high above her head and shoulder
Displaying perfect form as she slowly folds over

A talent or a gift she draws everyone in
Her body like water, flowing around each bend

Channeling her emotions as she wraps herself tight
Forming words with her body while making her spirit light

Seeing such beauty fills your heart to capacity
What a blessing that her dance alone can do that much for
Me

Hope is a Powerful Word

Hope; it means that at times you must let go
Holding on can raise you up or bring you low

Changing course when all seems lost
Opening yourself up without understanding the cost

Challenging what you know to be wrong
Pushing through life as you accept that you are strong

Hope provides a feeling of trust and expectation
Evolving into a need for something to happen that leads to a
Revelation

Hope is taking a chance that your needs will fall in place
Leading to a pleasing outcome without a fall from grace

Hope supports Faith when spoken from the heart
It's a powerful word, helping to hold together that which
Might come apart

Hope is where we wish others well when there's nothing else
To say
Hope is where we call out 'goodbye' when we really want to
Stay

Hope is where all want others to see who they are
Hope is the belief that salvation isn't very far

Hope is a powerful word with much to gain to meet your
Needs
Envision what you want… as you work diligently to succeed

Gone to Chase Butterflies (Ares)

Big, brown, smiling eyes
Love for your owner undisguised

Tail wagging with utter joy while entering the van
Excited to go for a ride but unable to stand

Your hind legs are dragging behind
Needing help from your friend who doesn't mind

Body feels odd and is refusing to comply
As you struggle to move with parts upon which you can no
Longer rely

Already missing your precious, silly face
Your friend is hurting with the decision to be made

He lays close to you in the van while whispering in your ear
Your friend of ten years now shedding tears

The veterinarian is patient, finally giving the injection with
Care
Your friend never leaving your side as you take your last
Breath of air

With memories of you, we all stand around and cry
Imagining you've gone home to chase butterflies

That silly basketball in your drooling mouth
Always appearing happy while running about

A family member is who you've always been
Our hearts are heavy with your loss and life's end

Cancer and arthritis came for you rapid in pace
You withstood it all with strength and grace

It hurt to watch each time you'd try
Wanting you to live forever and never die

Your beautiful black coat with hair shedding away
Your loss of appetite, your will to stay

The bread you'd accept as a special treat
Giving your friend hope when he felt defeat

You are so loved and missed, my friend
Gone to chase butterflies, now on four legs
Running again

Why Fall on a Sword?

Your role as you prepared for the call
You aren't expected to do it all

That job is taken
… If I'm not mistaken

Not everyone is filled with discontent
Some situations are not yours to represent

Have you noticed how often you want to make things right?
Perhaps everyone is required to fight their own fight

Lessons are how we learn
Your helpful actions prevent imminent returns

Why fall on a sword… can you survive?
Will you be there when needed, will you be alive?

A hero is not always what's sought
Listening is often the best reward for the distraught

Step back a moment and allow their strength to shine
Stop trying to save the world but continue to be kind

God is aware of all we say and do
His vision is not limited to only you

So, stand down and refocus your energy
Open your heart and allow yourself to see

You alone aren't expected to solve what's wrong
Remember, that job's taken, and his shoulders are strong

"Why fall on a sword?" A martyr can be a great loss
Decide to support others without using your life as the cost.

Willful Choice

God gave each of us the right to free will
We can choose to sustain life, or we can choose to kill

My choice in life is mine to make.
As is the decision of another to terminate

The conception of a child is a beautiful thing to behold
Rape, incest, illness, or the unknown can leave one
Unprepared for the role

It is not my place to tell another with an informed mind
What to do
They must decide for themselves what's best and choose to
Follow through

It is sad to think that any life is considered not worthwhile
However, death is inevitable, even that of a child

What has been done with removal of Roe versus Wade has
Created turmoil and a desire to fight
A few with power to redirect has taken away choices of
Others which was theirs by willful right

We don't all have to agree or even try to relate
Answering to God in the end is each of our final fate

Power can be like an unquenchable thirst
Leaving those wielding it with a desire to be first

Is it about making changes for those in need?
Or is it simply to fulfill the lives of those consumed by
Greed?

The choice to put aside a ruling against guns used to kill
Children in school
Appears to carry more credence for those chosen to do right
As a majority rule

The Golden Cage

If you are to live, you must first die
Your truth often follows your lie

Silence the voice wanting to set words free
Give thought to ideas that will be the key

Come into the warmth, out of the cold
Remember your youth as you grow old

Live in the present, having learned from the past
Never allow disagreements to linger or their shadows to last

Accept the wisdom that comes with age
Review your life's story and then turn the page

Slowly walk the path you once joyously ran
It's OK to do little when you've done all you can

We often look with hope and not always see
There's a golden cage, but we need to be free

Allow your heart to take the lead for the calm that you seek
Let your spirit be the guide as you find contentment and
Peace

There's much in life that is yet out of your control
The golden cage is convenient, but too weak for it to hold

Inner strength and determination have brought you far
Faith and the will to learn have made you who you are

At a Loss

Pacing back and forth like an animal in a cage
Youth now gone, replaced with age

Trying to form words that seem to take too much time
The conversation moves on, leaving you and your thoughts
Behind

Did you remember to eat or drink anything today?
Thoughts are so jumbled until your needs get in the way

Anger and frustration ever present, and you don't
Understand
You seek comfort from the use of the same words again and
Again

Unaware of the repetition, with your brain seemingly off
Track
Sometimes you go quiet, waiting for your initial thoughts to
Come back

You went for a walk this morning, but you forgot to get
Dressed
When asked if you were cold, giving a blank stare, you
Didn't confess

Watching as though through the eyes of a child
Saying little and yet giving your occasional smile

Speech becomes limited and self-care can be obsolete
Where once you were the lead, you're now feeling at a loss
In defeat

Forgetting how to dial on a phone or calling several times
The brain is so lost in the fog until it's unaware of the decline.

Frustration and unhappiness caused you to lash out for
Reasons you don't know.
Life and death cross paths but neither are clear on where to
Go

Reverting to childhood, you somehow have a fear
Independence is now gone, leaving behind a future that's
Devastating and unclear

Sharing long-forgotten memories to which others have no
Clue
Your loved ones feel sad watching over the stranger they no
Longer see as you

Lessons in Hate

There are those who say they represent the word of God our
Lord
And yet their lack of harmony hinders the presence of a
Pleasant chord

See God through prayer, allowing him to guide
Be aware that evil exists with nowhere to hide

Feelings that are stored up and held onto tightly will
Eventually come outside
The sisterhood and brotherhood experienced in comraderies
Have since died

Friendships held for over forty years are met with silence
And are now broken
Hate is encouraged, connections are torn apart with words
Never-before spoken

Men and women alike believe the painful and hurtful things
They say
There's so much discord tearing lives apart and into shreds
Every day

Who am I to accept a lie from someone giving voice to my
Hopes?
Following blindly as he offers a lifeline filled with falsehoods
To strengthen the rope

Getting on a ship filled with like-minds fulfills a long sought-
After need
Turning towards those giving credence to your frame of
Mind and away from those that disagree

Being carried forth with the crowd takes away the ability to
Think
The friendships initiated years ago once helped to strengthen
A long-established link

Once the ship is filled to capacity, will there be anyone to lift
You out?
Once it begins to sink can they hear your shout?

Friends of over forty years were all left stranded on Shore.
The ties to them over many years don't exist anymore

Hate will not save your life or listen when you have
Something to meaningful to say.
The ties were cut from years of connections in preparation
For this awful day

Looking across at those you'd left behind
Thoughts of the love, acceptance and joy once experienced
Finally cross your mind

As the ship slowly sinks…
You realize you miss the link

Those around you retain their hate
You cry out for forgiveness and pray it's not too late

Your Body Fights

Your body fights as your strength wanes
Your mind is full of images of red blood stains

Determined to stand on legs unable to bear the weight
The spirit is willing, but the weakened body knows it's too Late

Tears flow silently down the side of your face
There's no coming back from this dark place

You dare not put voice to your outcry for help
Your focus is on taking the predestined steps

There's no going back, you must think of where you are Without shame
You look for strength as you struggle to remember your Name

Running away is not the answer; this is your fight
Opening wide your arms you willingly accept your plight

Giving up was never an option as you prayed for what to do
A muffled voice of encouragement was guiding you through

The path wasn't straight, and the road was rocky and rough.
Your return was unsure, and you knew the healing would be
Tough

You believed this was a lesson and that you had to decide
Either accept what was offered or rely only on your pride

Many battles are fought and won with the acceptance of
Your needs
Letting go of your worries and troubles is when you are truly
Freed

A Loving Mother

The spirit of the child thrives in the heart of the mother
She loves her children like no other

Her touch is filled with love and care
She does for them what others would not dare

A mother's heart weeps when her child is in pain
She holds them tight as their fears wane

Their cards and flowers negate anything they've done wrong
She keeps their precious gifts to look at long after they're
Gone

A loving mother knows her child will make mistakes
She knows it's necessary to encourage them as much as it
Takes

A loving mother knows that a child must experience life as
Lessons learned
Sometimes things will go well and sometimes they'll get
Burned

A mother's love is steady and forever pure
When she faces challenges, she stands strong knowing she'll
Endure

A mother's love helps the child to stay grounded as they
Seek success
She remains available in their lives for when they need a
Home to return to for rest

A mother's supportive heart grows stronger as she holds
Back her fears
She cries alone as she watches her child struggle throughout
the years

She waits on the sidelines as they face their challenges
Wanting desperately to help.
A mother knows when to stay back because her child must
Take the next step

She's taught them how to get up when the struggle seems to
Keep them down
A mother teaches a child independence and self-preservation
For when she's no longer around

A mother's love for her child cannot compare
Her love and compassion make sure they know she'll always
Be there

That Smile

Holding onto memories that shadows have cast
Seeing her again after forty years gone past

Looking through the timelines for the sweet child
Reflecting on the memories of her precious smile

Hardships and life trials tried to beat her down
She fought back, dropping the chains that kept her bound

The pride I feel when looking upon her beautiful face
Reminds me of the day I left in such great haste

I knew I needed to get away
I felt bad knowing she had to stay

She was the youngest living in the home at the time
Her spirit was so bright and her smile so kind

Perhaps in forgetting at such a young age
She was able to start fresh once out of the cage

There was much she didn't know, leaving her unprepared
For the pain
She knew she'd done the right thing as she stumbled while
Running in the rain

It took years for her to gather the strength to get away
She'd been there too long but now she knew she couldn't
Stay

The abuse she experienced at the hands of that man made
Me sick to the core.
Such a beautiful spirit beaten down by a wolf in the sheep's
Clothing he wore

Her smile and laughter have cautiously returned as she
Grows into herself
She brings joy to those in her life, while strengthening the
Resolve she has left

The college education she wanted so badly became her
Reality
She set goals to achieve as she foresaw the woman she
Wanted to be

Her career is filled with daily challenges she meets with that
Smile
When reflecting on her past shadows, she still reminds me of
That precious child

Death Against Life

Death is always on time, never late
It doesn't understand love and hate

Death won't leave without its claim
It doesn't know your face or name

Death knows when the call is true
It will not hesitate to take what it's due

Death carries no darkness or light
It doesn't step in until there's acceptance without fight

Death seems calm as it transports with ease
It doesn't come to upset or to displease

Death is often burdened with a heavy load
It never fails to stay on the narrow road

It shows no discretion between enemy or friend
It has no consideration for pleas and no ability to mend

Death has no feelings and shows no emotion
It has no connections, therefore no devotion

Death waits patiently for the decision of free will.
It can't stop the action or interfere with the kill

Death has no control over life in the end
It collects what's left once life transcends.

Pity Pot

There's a long line for the pity pot
Dry your eyes, wipe away your snot

Gather up your britches and tighten your belt
This isn't the worst you've ever felt

There were times when the pain ran deep
You'd stayed awake when you wanted to sleep

Nobody is waiting to take your burdens away
Do something different or your demons will stay

Poor me, you think, I have it bad
Life was once happy but now it's sad

Looking in all the wrong places to quench your thirst
The last place you looked should have been the first

Climbing from a hole with no one to give you a hand
Crawling and stumbling until you're able to stand

What's the real reason behind your fate?
You took a wrong turn but it's not too late

You had a day where nothing went right
No longer determined, you gave up the fight

There's a long line for the pity pot.
Looks like no one saved your spot.

Put on your big-girl panties, there is much to do
Create an outlook on life with a better view

Follow the vein inside where your strength runs deep
The pot of gold at the end is yours to keep

Life will sometimes have challenges that make you want to
Run and hide
Roll up your sleeves and move forward with pride

The ups and downs are meant to be
Never giving up is what sets you free

Grandma Gertrude and the Wind

Don't stand alone when you can be with me
The words from the wind seemed to set me free

Put on your jeans and your favorite shirt
Let's chase the leaves and play in the dirt

Up and down the leaves flow across the field
I joyfully drop to the ground, watching as they settle and
Grow still

My thoughts are of Grandma Gertrude and all that she did
She was the calm and peace in my life when I was a kid

I miss her loving arms and the soothing stories she told
The wind reminds me that someday I too will grow old

Like the wind, Grandma Gertrude carried me along with
Patience and care
I hold onto the memories left behind, wishing she were still
There

The wisdom and subtle lessons she often instilled with grace
Are returned by the wind as the tears flow down my face

With thoughts of the unseen strength that she held in her
tiny frame
The wind reminds me of her many gifts left behind as it
Whispers her name

Grandma Gertrude's life wasn't easy, but she worked hard
And gave all she had
Family was everything to her and, like the wind, she gathered
Up the good with the bad

The wind goes away, returning to cover the earth with leaves
And in winter blowing the snow
Like our Grandma Gertrude, we never felt alone when she
Left, even though we knew she had to go

The Gift of You… A Second Chance

He took a visit that was well worth the view
He lived his life while cherishing you

Support through your love helped to sustain the fight
You both took a chance as you held on tight

No one should be alone when there's an opportunity to
Reconnect
Pain often runs deep but inner strength keeps your mind
From regret

Hold on to both sets of memories with all your heart
Know that in simply being you, you did your part

A second chance at love opened your heart times two
The companionship was unexpected, but you made do

Let not your heart be broken with yet another called away
Tears of pain remind you of your Loves who could not stay

An Angel of God and a shadow filled with grace
You never turned away from the challenges you were called
To face

A heart filled with kindness, compassion, and gentle care
When called to help, you willingly stepped forward to share

Through the eyes of your loves, you chose to give
So much of yourself freely shared to help them live

It was an honor to have received your care and love
They each now regard you through the veil of heaven above

You're their Angel on earth and so worthy of their time
Spent
A single day in your arms could never disclose how much
The years meant

There was no expectation of 'thank you' as your gentle care
Did proceed
You took your precious time doing for each, whatever you
Felt was their need

Once the deep threat of your grief slowly subsides,
Hold true to the fond memories of the two who were
Honored to walk at your side

Bring on your sunny smile that guides others through their
Day
The gift of 'you' made it difficult to leave when they so
Desperately wanted to stay

Ingram Content Group UK Ltd.
Milton Keynes UK
UKHW010113300623
424323UK00001B/3